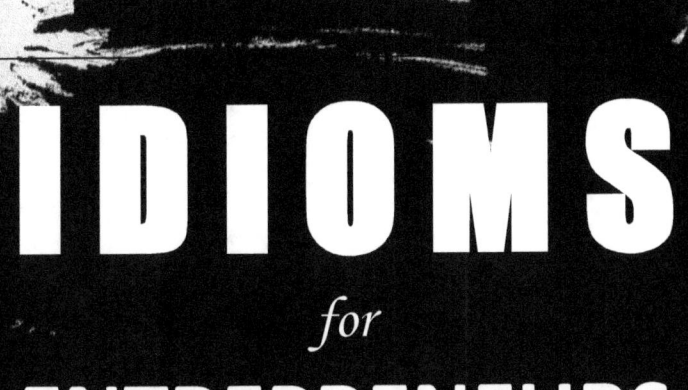

IDIOMS

for

ENTREPRENEURS

100 SAYINGS, PROVERBS, &
LESSONS FOR BUDDING
ENTREPRENEURS

JEREMY SKOOG

The advice in this book is intended to be helpful, inspirational, friendly, and taken with a grain of salt. Entrepreneurship journeys vary, and the experiences written here may be different as experienced from person to person, and business to business. As with any advice, the author does not assume any liability for loss or damage caused by interpretations of this writing (I do not know how it could, but you never know). You have a brain, use it to the best of its ability.

Copyright © 2021 Jeremy Skoog

Paperback: 978-1-4583-9317-3
Ebook: 978-1-7363271-1-1

Introduction

The English language is filled with thousands of idioms, sayings, and colloquialisms. These phrases usually have secondary meanings, apart from what their constituent words actually mean. These hidden meanings can be stories, proverbs, warnings, or just a concise way to say something complex.

We say them over and over to each other for years and years, each one able to be used in countless scenarios. Even though there are numerous applications for certain idioms, some of them and their hidden meanings are best applied to entrepreneurship, which is why this book exists... but more on that in a minute...

Entrepreneurship is such a complex process, and it is not a one size fits all experience. Each person will go through their own trials and tribulations, figure out their own solutions, and carry out business as each sees fit. Customers will react differently, business models and services differ, financial situations and outside help will differ. And even reading this book now, you might be at a completely different stage of entrepreneurship as the next person reading it.

But through all these differences, there is a common core in the entrepreneur's journey-- a "conventional wisdom" per say. And we can all draw from that collective wisdom in some capacity. Knowledge has been primarily passed through word of mouth and language for most of human history. Not only literally at face value, but with subtext hidden meaning. And this is where idiom's come in! Little bits of language that store and share wisdom in some capacity.

That's where this book comes in to play. Idioms may be generic, but they are still basically quick lessons and are easy to remember. So, by pairing them with some entrepreneurial knowledge we have quick, memorable lessons to dwell on. Perfect for reading when you are say... on the bus, or in the dentist lobby, or on the toilet, making every minute more productive and meditative!

It has been shown that the way you speak influences the way you think, thereby skewing your perception of the world, and yourself, in various ways. We say these idiom's all the time, so by pairing them with thoughtful entrepreneurial aspects, we can better mentally handle all the business hurdles thrown our way. It makes it easier to walk the walk and talk the talk!

So, take and read this book as it is, small bite sized tidbits and tips, filled with the personal and conventional experiences of others past, but not in one big gulp. Read some here, read a few there. Flip to random pages. Think of how the idioms compare to your own experiences, and how you can better steel yourself for success down the road.

Use these small moments as a time for introspection. After all, knowing yourself is the beginning of all wisdom.

The road to successful entrepreneurship is extremely difficult, but numerous people have had great success with it. A strong willpower and a thoughtful approach can take you a long way.

"I know for sure what we dwell on is who we become."

-Oprah Winfrey

1 "A journey of a thousand miles begins with a single step"

The entrepreneurial road is a long and hard one, but it is extremely rewarding and satisfying. It is the dream of many people: being your own boss, setting your own schedule, freedom to take time when you need it, not when it's granted. Indeed, there are many obstacles and hurdles that need to be overcome and sometimes the whole idea of it all can be overwhelming, but you'll never get there if you don't try. If you really want something you must go after it, it won't fall in your lap. Sometimes the hardest part of it all is taking the first step, but as you keep going it gets easier and easier, and soon you're walking at full speed (maybe even running).

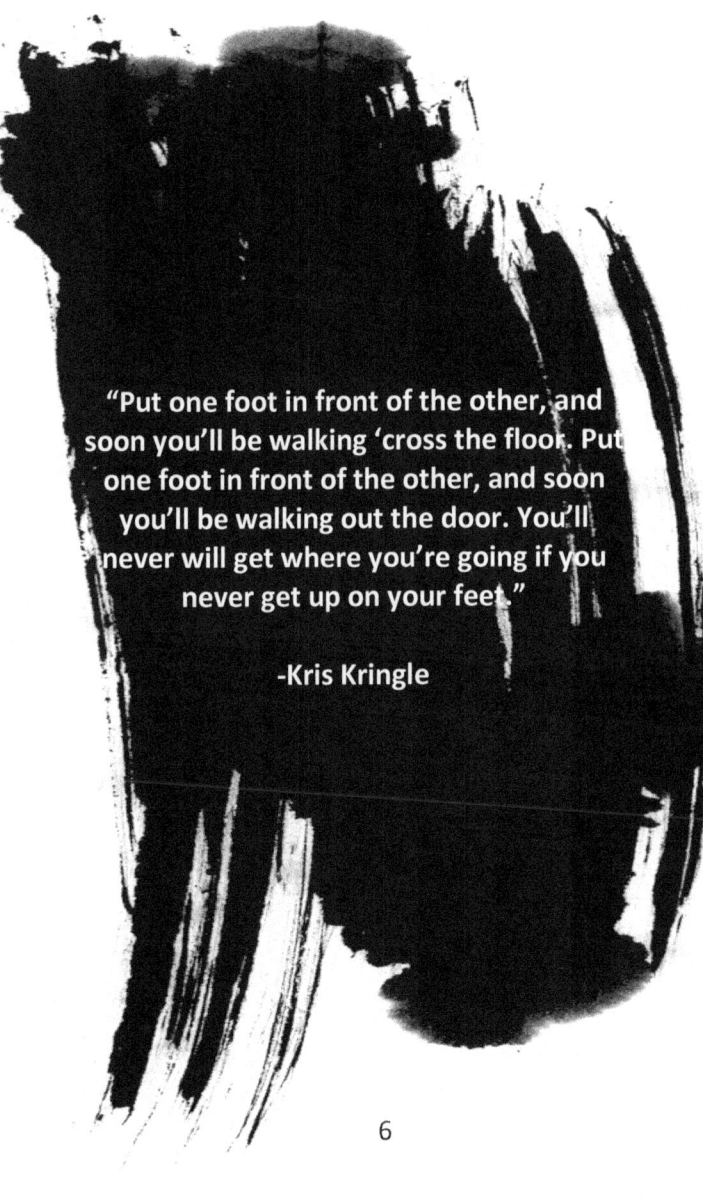

"Put one foot in front of the other, and soon you'll be walking 'cross the floor. Put one foot in front of the other, and soon you'll be walking out the door. You'll never will get where you're going if you never get up on your feet."

-Kris Kringle

2 "Better late than never"

3 "Never say never"
4 "Never too old to learn"
5 "Showing up is half the battle"

Everyone is on their own path in life. Just because you might reach milestones at a different time in your life than others doesn't mean you've failed in any way. If your path is leading you towards starting a business, there's no time like the present. Go after your dreams no matter how old you are! You will learn more about yourself, you will grow, you will learn. As the most interesting man once said, "It's never too late to start beefing up your obituary." Plus, "Founder and CEO" look good on a resume!

"It's never too late to start beefing up your obituary."

-The Most Interesting Man in the World

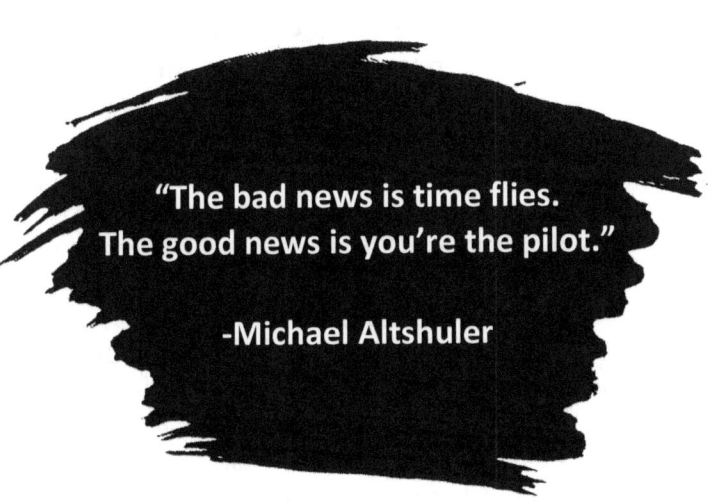

"The bad news is time flies.
The good news is you're the pilot."

-Michael Altshuler

6 "Easier said than done"

7 "Talk is cheap"
8 "Actions speak louder than words"
9 "Well done is better than well said"

It's easy to talk about being an entrepreneur and starting or running a business. A lot of people can do that, and even sound like they run a successful business. But a business is not just sounding like a business, at the end of the day it has to produce something! When you start down the path of entrepreneurship, it can sound like it's going to be an easy journey. When we talk about the steps necessary we don't realize, or even comprehend, all the work, effort, and skill that some tasks take. By actually doing things, checking them off the to-do list, producing product, we validate our words and our business. Realize that it is going to take a lot more work than you initially think, and attack it head on.

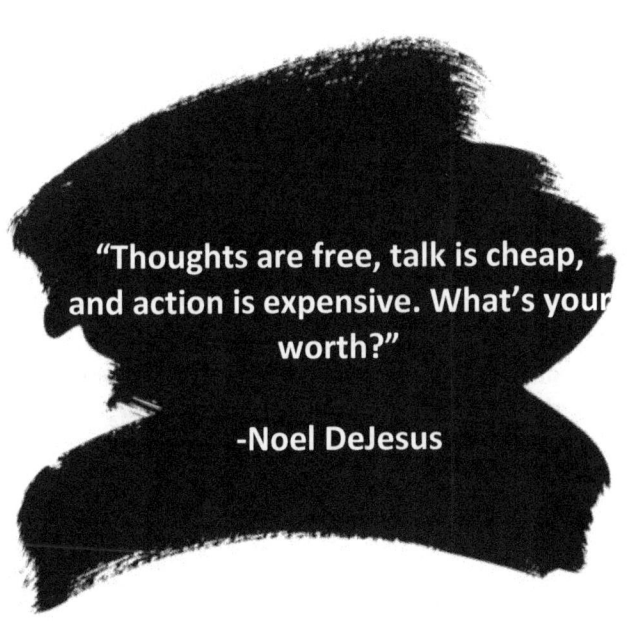

"Thoughts are free, talk is cheap, and action is expensive. What's your worth?"

-Noel DeJesus

10 "If at first you don't succeed, try, try again"

11 "What doesn't kill you makes you stronger"

Starting a business is no small undertaking, and it is fraught with hurdles, speed bumps, and obstacles. Chances are you're going to fail somewhere along the line, whether it's on an individual task, a product, or a whole business. But it's okay! Failure is always an option, and it's an amazing teacher. "Fail fast, fail often" can be a great way to learn and quickly weed out what's working and what's not, and you can benefit from the experience in the future. Learning how to handle failure and setbacks in an important part of entrepreneurial life-- and keeping a positive mindset can work wonders for you and your productivity.

"Do or do not. There is no try."

-Yoda

12 "Failing to plan is planning to fail"

13 "Look before you leap"

When you make up your mind and are ready to dive into starting a business, it can be really exciting, and you can't wait to go all in. But first you need a plan. A plan that you should spend a fair amount of time putting together too. You don't build a mansion off the top of your head, why would you do the same with your baby business?

Come up with a business plan. Figure out your ideal customer, how are you going to reach them? Marketing, how will people find your business? How exactly is your product produced? What costs and bills will you have to pay? How much money will you have to make per month? Can you ease into it with part time work? Consider as many aspects of your business as possible. The more you account for and plan for, the better chances you'll have of succeeding.

"A goal without a plan is a wish."

14   "Fake it 'til you make it"

15   "Respect is not given, it is earned"

It is hard building up a reputation for a business, especially when you're just starting out. People don't want to get scammed or conned by some no-name company, they want value for their hard-earned money. So first you must ensure that you are providing the best value that you can. Don't cut corners you shouldn't, and don't make false promises, and your customers will start to understand your value proposition more and more and you progress. All the while, clearly and confidently advertise your value as a mature and established business. If you talk big and back it up with results, your customers will respect you more and more.

"Don't fake it 'til you make it. Own it while you hone it."

-Christer Kaitila

16 "A smooth sea never made a skilled sailor"

Chances are it's not going to be smooth sailing on your entrepreneurial journey. There are so many countless things that can and will go wrong. You will make mistakes. You will have struggles. But take heart, as each of these is an opportunity to learn and to perfect your skills as a businessperson.

Sure, rough times aren't fun while you're in them, but you will be better off in the long run having experienced them, rather than without.

"You always pass failure on the way to success."

-Mickey Rooney

17 "Fortune favors the bold"

18 "God helps those who help themselves"
19 "No guts, no glory"
20 "Nothing ventured-
-nothing gained"
21 "Risk it for the biscuit"
22 "No risk, no reward"

Not everyone appreciates a good idea. Some people may think it's dumb, others may think it can't be done, or maybe others don't want to see you try at all (Either for fear of failure, or fear of success). But sometimes you'll have a gut feeling that just can't be ignored, and you should give it a shot. Just because something may be expensive, or risky, or unknown, doesn't mean it should be ignored. No one ever succeeded greatly by daring slightly.

At some point you're going to have to take calculated risks, because that's where a lot of the reward is. Whether that's investing in something different, launching a totally different product, or even quitting your day job to pursue entrepreneurship full time. It might not turn out the way you intended, but you'll never know for certain if you don't try.

"There is only one big risk you should avoid at all costs, and that is the risk of doing nothing."

-Denis Waitley

23 "Where there's a will, there's a way"

24 "Whether you think you can, or you think you can't, you're right"

Your mindset is one of your greatest assets in life, let alone entrepreneurship, but it can also be one of the biggest hindrances as well. It can be easy to think and even be overwhelmed by negative thoughts, and these will weigh you down over time, and eventually defeat you. But a positive mindset, optimistic thinking, and faith in yourself and your abilities can work wonders. You will be able to overcome huge obstacles you never thought possible because if you truly want something and believe it can be achieved, you have what it takes to make it a reality.

"Nothing is impossible. The word itself says 'I'm possible!'"

-Audrey Hepburn

25 "No man is an island"

26 "Two heads are better than one"

Starting and running a business is extremely difficult, but you don't have to go it alone. There are great benefits of sharing the load and working with other people. Perhaps you know someone who would make a great business part and shares similar goals? Even if you don't want to part control of your business to a partner, you could consider contracting out to freelancers or other companies to assist you with the workload. Sure, these cost money (which for a startup is a very precious commodity), but the time savings alone could more than make up for it, especially if you aren't as skilled in certain areas.

Additionally, meeting up with fellow entrepreneurs and business owners can be a great way to learn, trade ideas, and commiserate. There are often groups with monthly meetups that you can join in and meet new, likeminded people.

27 "Tell me who your friends are, and I'll tell you who you are"

28 "Birds of a feather flock together"

They say that you are the average of the five people you spend the most time with. This is because your personalities, thoughts, and ideas all rub off on each other. It can sometimes be hard to hear it, but sometimes the people you choose to spend time with are indirectly holding you back. Are people particularly negative all the time? Pessimistic? These things can permeate to you and negatively affect your mindset. Is there anyone around you that is too much of a time sink, or is overly needy? Building a business takes hundreds if not thousands of hours of dedicated time to create. These are not hard fast rules by any means so don't just ditch your friends because a book said so. But they are things to consider on your journey, and maybe some relationship adjusting is required. Be mindful of the effect different people have on you, whether for better or worse.

29 "You cannot win them all"

Not every product you create will be a roaring success, and you will not turn every prospective buyer into a customer. It's impossible. Repeat after me: no one has a perfect track record! Not even Nike or Apple or Lamborghini or any big name brand have a perfect track record. Everyone must accept defeat in a battle every once in a while. But there is always the next one. Keep trying! Try new ideas, new concepts, and never be afraid of failure! And if a customer is just putting you through the wringer again and again, giving you more grief than you can handle, drop the customer! You don't need (or want) every single person to be a customer.

"Sometimes you win, sometimes you learn."

30   "Divide and conquer"

It can be daunting looking at your mountain of tasks on your to do list, and some of your projects and goals may seem insurmountable. Even though as a whole some things might take weeks, months, or years to accomplish, (and it is good to realize this and be okay with it) trying to tackle the whole thing at once will do you a disservice and can hurt your mental state.

But you've got to get it done. One of the best ways to overcome large tasks is to break it down to smaller components, and complete each one individually. Taking consistent small steps is better than inconsistent big ones for several reasons:

• Smaller tasks are easier and quicker to complete than larger ones.

- Working consistently can keep your momentum up, which will help you in the long haul.

- By completing small tasks, you mentally feel more achieved than half completing something, thereby keeping you in a stronger mental state.

"Be not afraid of growing slowly, be afraid only of standing still."

-Chinese Proverb

34 "Don't count your eggs before they've hatched"

Before you've taken the plunge into full time self-employment, don't accidentally overestimate the value of your new venture. Even though optimism is essential for any budding business person, until you're actually selling a product (and turning a profit), any revenue projection is all just theoretical. Don't plan on a theoretical income to sustain you immediately. Many businesses take years before they return a sustainable income.

You definitely need a healthy dose of confidence though, but it needs to be a pragmatic confidence.

"Don't count your chickens before they hatch… unless you want eggs. In that case, carry on."

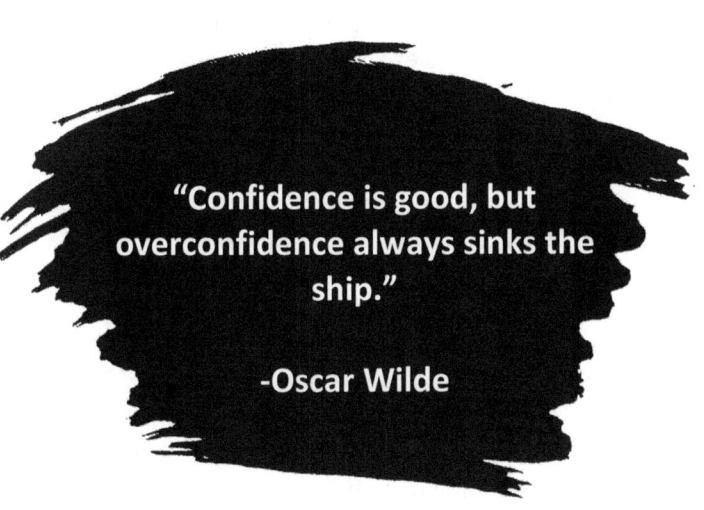

"Confidence is good, but overconfidence always sinks the ship."

-Oscar Wilde

35 "Cross that bridge when you come to it"

When you're planning future business ventures, you often are trying to predict a number of variables and future expenses. What tools will I need? What software should I buy? How much initial product should I stock? As much as you might want the latest and greatest software or the newest top of the line machinery, all of this takes money, money that might be better used elsewhere. What can happen is you'll convince yourself that in the future you'll need something to solve a specific problem or make your life easier, you buy it, use it twice, and then it sits idly the rest of its life because plans changed. Or the time and money it saves will only pay off the tool after 10 years of service! That is a long time to be in the red for not much value! It is better to wait until a problem actually arrives before you find a solution to it.

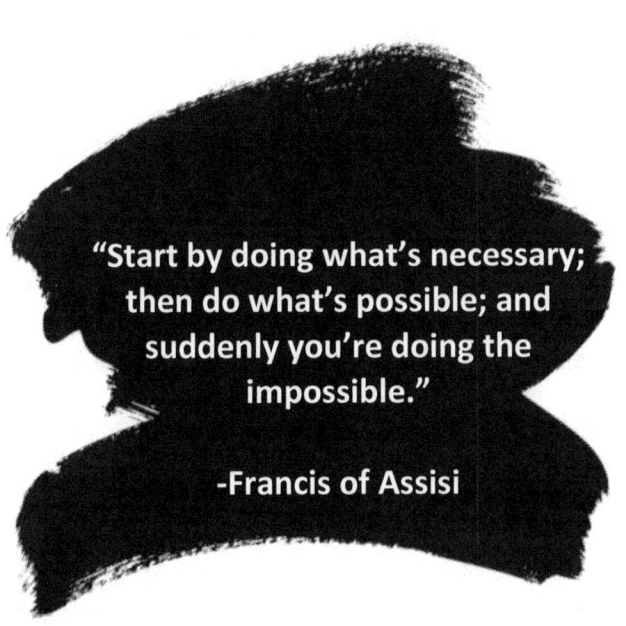

"Start by doing what's necessary; then do what's possible; and suddenly you're doing the impossible."

-Francis of Assisi

36 "Go big or go home"

37 "Put your best foot forward"

With so many different businesses out there and the number of entrepreneurs growing every year, every single market is becoming more and more saturated. With so much competition, it is essential that you differentiate yourself from everyone else in order to be noticed and succeed. If everyone is providing identical value, it's just a random chance that you get picked by the customer (or price is the deciding factor). To increase your odds of success, not only should your product be different or unique from the rest, but your customer service is better, your marketing is on point, anything you can do to stand out. It will take a lot more effort, but if this is your livelihood and something you really want to succeed in, why not go all out?

"Don't half-ass anything. Whatever you do, always use your full ass."

38 "You reap what you sow"

39 "If a job is worth doing, it's worth doing well"
40 "Go the extra mile"

If you don't put in the effort, don't expect great results. If you want to create top notch products to sell, you're going to have to put in top notch work to create them. If you want to run a top tier restaurant, you have to use top tier ingredients and recipes. Cutting corners, rushing tasks, and skipping out on details can come back and bite you later, making your life harder in the long run. If you take the time and do things correctly the first time, you will save your future self time down the road. Upfront effort can reward massively over a business's life.

"Work hard now. Don't wait. If you work hard enough, you'll be given what you deserve."

-Shaquille O'Neal

41 "If you want something done right, you've got to do it yourself"

42 "A picture paints a thousand words"

As much as you want to do everything yourself, there just isn't enough time in the day. Inevitably at some point, you'll be dealing with subcontractors. In doing so, it can sometimes be difficult to fully convey every little detail you need. You have your vision that you can even picture in your mind's eye. But it turns out, people can't read your mind. You may have an idea already in your head of what you want, but when you delegate, you relinquish a lot of control and creative freedom. If it is important that your vision is met to your exacting specifications, you need to take extra time and care to carefully relay as much information as you can, and one of the best ways to convey information is visually with pictures, diagrams, sketches, technical drawings, etc. Even if you're not an artist, putting blobs on paper and labeling them is better than nothing!

43 "Patience is a virtue"

44 "A watched pot never boils"
45 "Good things come to those who wait"
46 "Rome wasn't built in a day"

Building a business is a long, tedious, and sometimes boring path, and it can be frustrating when you don't see immediate fruits of your efforts. But it really does take a long time to get up to speed and to start getting traction in the marketplace. You have to be mentally prepared for a slow start, especially if you are developing a product. Everything will take longer than you expect. EVERYTHING. Steel yourself to that fact, be patient, and you will make it through.

"There are no shortcuts. Only hard work. Train hard and be patient. It will pay off."

47 "The early bird gets the worm"

48 "First come, first served"
49 "If you can't be on time, be early"

If you're in the habit of showing up late, turning in homework late, responding to customer emails late, you might want to reconsider your life choices. It's seemingly such a trivial thing; what's the big deal being a few minutes late anyway? But it can have surprisingly detrimental consequences, especially for business, for a few reasons.

First, humans experience a mental effect known as "anchoring." This is a phenomenon in which someone usually perceives the first thing they see in a group as superior in some way. So if your fall marketing is late, someone might think your sweater is slightly inferior than the one they saw an ad for yesterday, and you don't want that!

Secondly, when paying customers don't get what they expect on time, they begin to worry, and our minds often wander to the worst-case scenarios. Did my package get lost? Did they take my money and run? This can be alleviated with good communication, but why make your customers more stressed out? Conversely, when customers get the value that they are paying for when they expect it, or even earlier than expected in the best case, they experience a large mental positivity boost towards your business. This won't affect you immediately, but over time as you build up a reputation, prospective customers will be more inclined to spend their hard-earned cash with you over someone else who is perpetually late.

People have been hired and fired for being minutes early and late respectively, and customers won't hesitate to drop businesses based on their delivery schedules. Don't let that happen to you.

50 "You can't manage what you don't track"

This speaks for itself! If you're not keeping records or metrics of things, how are you supposed to know how things are trending? Which product sells best which month? Where are additional expenses piling up? Which marketing ad converts more? Google/YouTube, Facebook/Instagram, Apple, have all grown huge in no small part that they can keep extremely detailed metrics on their users and their behavior. While you might not be able to tap into your customer's phone like they can, you still have useful data that you can learn from-- if you track it appropriately and consistently.

51 "The customer is always right"

52 "The customer is king"

A business only exists if it can provide value or service to customers in some way. If that's not happening, then there is no revenue stream, and a business won't last long without that. That is paramount to running a successful business. Happy customers will tell their friends about your product and create great word of mouth marketing. This means you might have to work a little harder to make some customers happy. You might have to take a loss on some sales due to change orders, wrong sizes, shipping losses, etc. But that's okay, as overall you should still be turning a profit.

As an entrepreneur, and especially as a fee for service contractor, you have a little more flexibility with this. You can choose your customers to some extent. If a customer is getting too hard to handle, or if dealing with them is not worth the benefit of having them, you are allowed to drop them if necessary. (But make sure you are not ripping them off or screwing them over if you do! Be courteous!)

53 "When life gives you lemons, make lemonade"

54 "Every cloud has a silver lining"

As failures are inevitable in every venture, a lifelong skill is to be able to face them, accept them, learn from them, and move on. But one of those is the most important one of the batch: learn from failure. Something's going to fail. You cannot stop it from happening. But all is not lost in failure. You can gain knowledge, improve a skill, know what to look out for when you try next time.

55 "Jack of all trades, master of none"

As an entrepreneur, you're going to have to get used to the fact that you are required to wear many hats. You might be the CEO, machinist, bookkeeper, shipping specialist, and customer support rolled into one snazzy unit. You're also going to have to get used to the fact that you initially might not know how to do all those jobs, and that you won't be the best at all of them. And that's okay! You will always learn more and get better as you go along, and at some point you may even subcontract out the jobs that you're not the best at.

Secondly, people like to say this phrase like it's a rule or something. You can master multiple things, and you probably will! If you learn self-control, you can master anything.

"I'm not a jack of all trades; I'm a master of many. I don't feel there is anything I can't do if I want to."

-Evel Knievel

56 "Haste makes waste"

57 "Don't jump the gun"
58 "Measure twice, cut once

Don't be afraid to take a little extra time on something when needed. By holding off pulling the trigger you can avoid mistakes, oversights, and poor decisions. If you're not sure about something, don't make a decision on it right then and there. If you don't know if a purchase is a good investment or asset, sleep on it. If you can't remember the next step in a process, look it up before proceeding. Taking your time and ensuring you do things as correct as possible the first time will save you time, money, and grief down the road.

59 "What goes around comes around"

60 "You are what you eat"

The effort and care you put in will reflect on the finished business or product. If you skimp on certain details here or there, someone will notice them, and might think less of your product in the future. Obviously you can't make a perfect product, but the work and effort you put into something will show in the end.

Similarly, this applies to marketing and business relations as well. If you build and curate quality relationships, you will be reciprocated in such. Help other small entrepreneurs as you try to build your own business, and communally you might be able to grow larger than you could alone. Cross-promotions are a great way to expand your market reach!

61 "There's more than one way to skin a cat"

62 "Think outside the box"

One pitfall many people fall into is the idea that things have to be done precisely a certain way. While there is indeed conventional wisdom on why things are done in a particular manner, you often do yourself a disservice locking yourself into that mentality. Whether this is requiring the top notch tools of the trade, only buying one particular premium brand of something, or only doing A before B, when you're starting out it may not be the best for you. You could be spending way more money than necessary or overthinking things and wasting time when there might be cheaper or simpler alternatives that provide similar (but still satisfactory) results. Sometimes your ego or training or mindset is making things harder than they need to be.

63 "Don't give up the day job"

64 "Don't put all your eggs in one basket"

Optimism and confidence are usually present in overwhelming quantities in the early stages of your entrepreneurship journey, and both are totally essential for success! Unfortunately, these can often blind you to many of the upcoming hurdles and pitfalls that are in your way. As much as you may want to dive in headfirst and give it everything you've got, it might be better (or safer) to start your entrepreneur journey as a side gig to another job, whether it's full or part time work. This way you still have a safety net and a steady income that can help pay for your new business venture, and keep you living if your venture inevitably takes longer to get off the ground and turn a profit than you planned. Income from new businesses is the furthest thing from steady, so it's one way to make sure you don't run out of cash.

65 "Don't try to walk before you can crawl"

It's simple to see what other businesses are doing and say to yourself, "That looks pretty easy, I think I can do that easily too!" But it's a trap. What we don't often see is all the hard work, planning, pitfalls, trial and error, research, and time that goes into an end result. To doing anything there is a learning curve and some tribal knowledge, or hidden nuances, that must be understood first. So, to accomplishing anything you must make sure you readily understand the smaller steps involved in any process, before tackling larger ones. Secondly, make sure that your current projects are working and profitable before tackling other, seemingly simple ones.

66 "Kill two birds with one stone"

As an entrepreneur and running your own business, there is going to be no shortage of tasks for you to do. In the early stages, most likely being a company of one, you're going to have to do everything yourself; marketing, documentation, customer service, taxes, listings, copy... let alone making and shipping a product. It is important then to consider your time and your effort as precious commodities as well. There is only so much you can do in a day! But by taking a small amount of extra time, effort, planning, and patience, you will find that you can often compound multiple tasks into one, saving you all the aforementioned greatly down the line. These could be things such as buying a tool that will work for multiple projects or creating advertising media that will work on the web, in print, and social platforms. Or maybe it's updating your FAQ that solves active customer issues, or utilizing tools that can consolidate and handle all your social media accounts in one place. Stretching your efforts to cover multiple tasks will pay dividends over time.

67 "Less is more"

Your inner perfectionist will tell you that your business must have the best packaging, the best website, the best user experience, the best functionality, the best advertising, and so on and so forth. But if you try to accomplish all of these things at the beginning, your business will never even get started! In the early days, it is important to sell your product and get it out the door with the least amount of resistance from yourself. You can add better packaging, better advertising, better pictures as you go along, but it is so important that you start turning a profit early.

Decide what your core necessities are to get a minimum viable product out the door are, and trim any "wants" that you can have in the future, but are not necessary now. "Wants" take time and cost money, your two most valuable assets in business. The less of those you spend getting your product out the door, the more of both you'll have!

68 "Don't put off until tomorrow what you can do today"

69 "There is no time like the present"

Not every task is the most exciting, stimulating, or rewarding thing to do, and we tend to push those ones off further and further down the road. But if they do need to be done, why not complete them sooner than later? If you have the time and ability to accomplish something now, by actually doing it now you further progress down the road towards the main objective and you free up some future time for more pressing issues (that will inevitably arrive). By putting things off, you just prolong the inevitable; the overall time you spend will just increase, future projects will happen further in the future. It all compounds over time into a larger waste of time.

Parkinson's Law

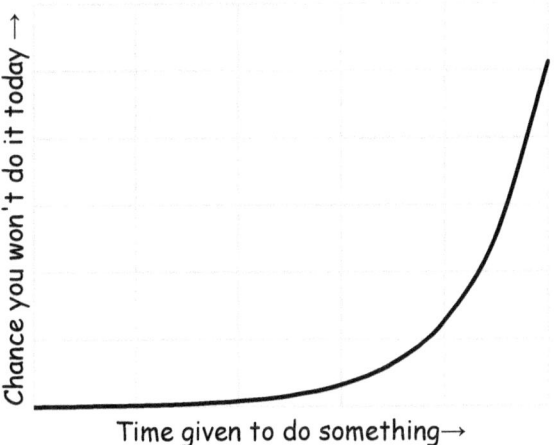

Ideal Procrastination

How much work you have

How much you procrastinate

Real Procrastination

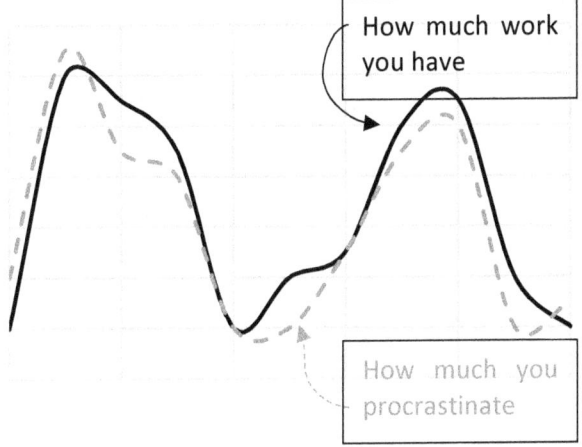

70 "Strike when the iron is hot"

When you are motivated or interested in a certain task or project, it's ok to work on it if you have some spare time (even if it's not the top priority). When truly motivated, you'll be amazed at how much you can accomplish in a small amount of time. It's like a productivity multiplier! Use it to your advantage to get things done. They say that 90% of a project can be completed in the same amount of time as the last 10%, so with motivation it can be really easy to complete that first 90% and get yourself halfway there in the shortest amount of time.

"Do it now. Sometimes 'later' becomes 'never.'"

71 "You'll never get if you never go"

So, you've been tossing around the idea of starting a business, writing a book, starting a YouTube channel, or taking on any new venture, for a while now but there is just so much that could go wrong, or it might not work out or there's too many obstacles in the way. If you've been thinking about anything like that for any length of time, stop just thinking and start doing!

"Don't let your dreams be dreams. Just do it!"

-Shia LaBeouf

72 "Easy come, easy go"

Along the difficult road of entrepreneurship and running a business, remember that there are other entrepreneurs just like you that have many of the same struggles, hardships, and ambitions. If you have some success, be sure to share some of it with your peers. Not only by supporting their business with the occasional purchase, but by spreading the word about them, helping them with advice (if they ask for it), and supporting their efforts as well. It can be hard to go it alone, and maybe some comradery and a little help is all someone needs to move further along their journey as well. Remember, you can always make more money.

"Only by giving are you able to receive more than you already have."

-Jim Rohn

73 "Honesty is the best policy"

74 "Cheats never prosper"

Customers aren't stupid, and they do not exist to buy your product, so don't try to "pull a fast one" on them. If an interested customer uses your product frequently, they will find faults or what is lacking in it, and if it is a big enough inconvenience or annoyance to them, they will drop you like a sack of bricks and never come back. Customers want a reliable, safe and secure, business to interact with. They want to spend their money with good people, people they can trust, not jerks or cons. And they'll be on the lookout for anything suspicious as well. If they detect a warning sign or red flags anywhere, they'll be less likely to spend their money with you.

"The truth doesn't cost anything, but a lie could cost you everything."

75 "Hope for the best, prepare for the worst"

Optimism and a positive mindset are great assets during the entrepreneur journey. That's the whole reason to get in this business anyway: the hope to run a successful business and to create a living for yourself. But it is definitely not all sunshine and flowers, and you need to steel yourself for plenty of setbacks and failures. Having a backup plan, emergency funds, alternative business ideas, that you can resort to if needed can save your bacon when speed bumps occur.

"The idea of this line is that you have to balance those two things. Offence and defense. Feet on the ground, head in the clouds... dream big, but be okay if things don't work out.

-Itauber

76 "Knowledge is power"

77 "A little learning is a dangerous thing"

One core attribute to successful entrepreneurship and life in general is to never stop learning. Never ever! There is no point in your life when you will say "I know all there is to know about this." because the more you know about something, the more you realize you don't know about it.

As a new entrepreneur, there's going to be a lot that you don't know, and you might not even know it yet! You're going to have to learn new skills, new abilities, new methods and techniques that you never thought you would try, because it's probably just you at the beginning, and if you don't figure it out you probably won't get very far. An added bonus is that the more you know about different fields, the better you will be at coming up with fresh ideas and concepts. Struggling to solve a problem or come up with a new idea? Get out there and learn some new things, and a solution may present itself in a way you couldn't imagine!

78 "Hindsight is 20/20"

As you progress down the road of entrepreneurship, learning, practicing, gaining skills, gaining knowledge, it can be hard not to look behind you at some of the mistakes you've made along the way. Some pitfalls may seem so blatantly obvious now that it can be painful. You have to remember though that these difficulties and challenges brought you to where you are today. You have learned from them and you have more experience because of them. Sure, it would be nice if they wouldn't have happened, but they did, and here you are. So keep moving forward!

"Forgive yourself for not having the foresight to know what now seems so obvious in hindsight."

-Judy Belmont

79 "Time is money"

Money is oftentimes the primary metric used in business as it is very tangible, easy to track, and has immediate face value (literally!). And sometimes it can be easy to get caught up thinking that money is the *only* metric to track, especially in starting a new business. This goes hand in hand with the idea that most people horribly undervalue their own time, as well as underestimate the time it takes to accomplish things.

It is paramount to remember that the time you spend doing one task is time you can't spend doing another (humans can't actually multitask, we just like lying to ourselves). You also have to remember that after taking care of your business expenses, you have to pay yourself too! So it is important to determine the value of your time, and to determine what tasks are worth that value and what tasks are worth purchasing/subcontracting out. It can be difficult at first, as new businesses aren't overflowing with cash to throw around, and it's not going to work out all of the time. But once you get good at this skill, you will find you suddenly have superhuman productivity abilities, as you are freed up from lesser, cheaper tasks to focus on the larger, more expensive ones.

You only have a finite amount of time. Time is spent to make money. However you can't spend money to buy time, but you can buy somebody else's time with it.

"Time is what we want most, but what we use worst."

-William Penn

80 "You get what you pay for"

81 "Get the most bang for your buck"

It's always been difficult to quantify the exact amount of value you can get for an amount of money, as there are nearly an infinite amount of variables to consider. For any amount of value, someone can probably provide it for cheaper, but they're going to have to cut corners. Someone else might be particularly proud of their value, so they charge a lot more over average price. But how can you tell?

Typically the cost per value is an exponential curve, meaning that it costs more and more to make smaller and smaller value growths. Top of the line performance will have a pretty penny price tag. Cheap entry level items might not last long or leave something to be desired.

The more you know about a product or service, the better you will be able to judge a given price, so educate yourself before pulling the trigger. Maybe sleep on it and trust your gut. The real trick isn't knowing what's expensive and what's not, it's knowing what you need to spend more money on and what you don't. Remember the tradeoff: if you have good, fast, and cheap, you can only pick two.

Gain experience, gain knowledge, and know what you need. Then pay what it requires.

"It's unwise to pay too much, but it's worse to pay too little."

Cost and Value are Exponentially Related

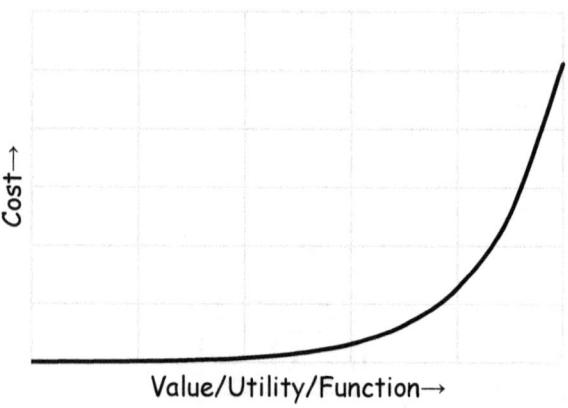

"If you think it's expensive to hire a professional to do the job, wait until you hire an amateur."

-83 oranges

82 "You can't make bricks without straw"

83 "Use the right tool for the job"

First, physically, you need the correct tools and materials to produce your product. Each tool is designed for a specific purpose, so choosing the correct tool will also decrease the amount of time and effort required to get a job done right. (The pros and cons of any given tool should also be weighed against its price, so make sure you come out ahead!)

Secondly, mentally, you need to continually educate yourself so that you have proper and adequate information and knowhow to produce the best product that you can. This can come from requesting feedback, testing, reviews, etc. The more you know about your product, it's use, it's ins and outs, and its lifecycle, the better the value you can contribute towards it.

84 "All work and no play makes Jack a dull boy"

85 "Business before pleasure"

These two idioms might seem like they're complete opposites of each other, but they actually tie well hand-in-hand.

Look, at the end of the day, entrepreneurship and running a business is tough. There are customers to keep happy, tasks to be completed, and work that needs to get done. If you want to progress and keep the ball rolling, you're going to have to prioritize some things in your life, and you might have to make some sacrifices. But it's not all that! Entrepreneurship and running your own business (running your own life) can be extremely rewarding and fun. Plus, it can allow for more scheduling freedom that can let you live your life on your terms, not constrained by arbitrary work hours. It's a balancing act for sure, but it's definitely doable.

"Don't give up what you want most for what you want now."

-Richard G Scott

86 "Work expands to fill the time available"

This saying, also known as Parkinson's Law, is something to keep in mind when you're scheduling and planning. This idea is basically if you have too much time for a project, you will think of new features or details to add, and the project will grow in complexity. Secondly, everybody procrastinates to some extent. If you know there is still time for you to work on something later, chances are you will put it off until later! Delays make the overall completion time for a task longer, which means you are less productive in the long run.

To overcome this, it is important to first understand and realize that this phenomenon does exists, and everyone is extremely prone to it. Then, follow some of these pointers:

- Identify the objectives or deliverables of a project or task

- Clarify roles and responsibilities of you or the people working on a task.

- Identify what is in and out of scope, and other restricting parameters

- Figure out what trade-offs are available. If something goes wrong, it's easier to decide what gets cut if it's been predefined.

- Outline a timeline, including milestones and deadlines, which can utilize the power of small wins to keep momentum up.

"We don't drift into good directions. We discipline and prioritize ourselves there."

-Andy Stanley

87 "Practice makes perfect"

88 "No pain no gain"

You're not going to be the best at everything you try. As an entrepreneur and business owner, you're going to have to juggle many hats and take on tasks that you've never tried before. Some will come naturally, others you will have to take time and put dedicated practice towards. They say it takes 10,000 hours of practice to be considered a master at something. That's almost 5 years of practice at 40 hours a week! But the great thing is, you don't have to be a master to be proficient at something!

Let's examine this. We know that as people get better at things, it gets increasingly harder to then improve more. Skill improvement is inversely exponential, or a logarithmic growth curve. Combine this with the 90/10 rule of management, the last 10 percent of anything will take 90 percent of the time. This means that you can be in the top 10 percent of a skill after only one thousand hours of practice (roughly half a year at 40 hours a week), and that you can be above average in a skill (being in the top 50%)

after only 3 months! And 3 months can go by so fast.

Practice. If you want to get better at something, you have to practice. And very rapidly, you'll be better at it than most people you know.

"Practice isn't the thing you do when you're good. It's the thing you do that makes you good."

-Malcolm Gladwell

89 "Back to the drawing board"

90 "Let's go back to square one"

Sometimes you're going to go down a path, make decisions, or release products that just don't pan out or aren't successful.

AND THAT'S OK!

It's all part of the learning process! Sometimes you can salvage what you've got, but other times it's more economical to reevaluate everything, come up with a new plan, and start over. Oftentimes the new direction you take will be better than the one you were on. Plus, this time you're not starting from scratch, you're starting from experience.

This might actually be a breath of fresh air as you will have new problems to solve, and usually the beginning of a new project is the most exciting part!

"Starting all over again is not that bad-because when you restart, you get another chance to get things right."

"I'm not giving up;
I'm just starting over."

91 "When the going gets tough, the tough get going"

Entrepreneurship is A LOT of hard work.

A. Lot. Of. Hard. Work. And there are going to be tons of hurdles, obstacles, and setbacks thrown your way, on a daily basis. And you might not have answers to your struggles right now either. On average in the first three years of operating, 33% of business will fail, and 33% will spin their wheels without gaining any traction, basically constituting a hobby. To be in the remaining third you will have to fend off blow after blow, setback after setback.

But if you really want it, if you REALLY WANT IT, you can weather the storm and find a route through your hurdles (it's also a never-ending storm, you just have to get used to it). Have faith, have courage, and be tough!

"When you're going through hell, keep going..."

-Winston Churchill

92 "The pen is mightier than the sword"

When dealing with subcontractors, something's going to go wrong. A part will come out the wrong size, the colors will be off, the font will be wrong, the picture might be too washed out... the list of things that can go wrong is endless. As a small business with tight budgets, it can be extremely frustrating when these problems arise, and you might feel let down, downtrodden, or even worse: betrayed. These are all-natural responses, as you had hopes and dreams and time and money riding on this. But before you do anything rash (like drop the contractor as revenge) send an email and describe your issues. Subcontractors are businesses too (often small-scale entrepreneurs like yourself), and they also want to make their customers happy. Maybe some details were overlooked or miscommunicated during the quoting process, or maybe certain requirements that are obvious to you are not obvious to the subcontractor. Chances are, they will want to work with you to solve the issue, and get you back on track.

93 "The squeaky wheel gets the grease"

In order for your business to flourish, you need to bring in potential customers. Unfortunately for you, unless you provide life saving value, they will not seek you out. So you need to get out there and make yourself known. Make some noise, do some marketing, do a publicity stunt, start an Instagram account, tell the world about the value you provide! It will take an upfront investment of time and money, and your first few attempts may not yield much, but you will learn and get better and progress.

People aren't likely to buy something the first time they see an ad either. You must first *plant the seed*, then nurture it with a follow up stream of ads, information, posts, etc. in order to convert potential customers into paying customers.

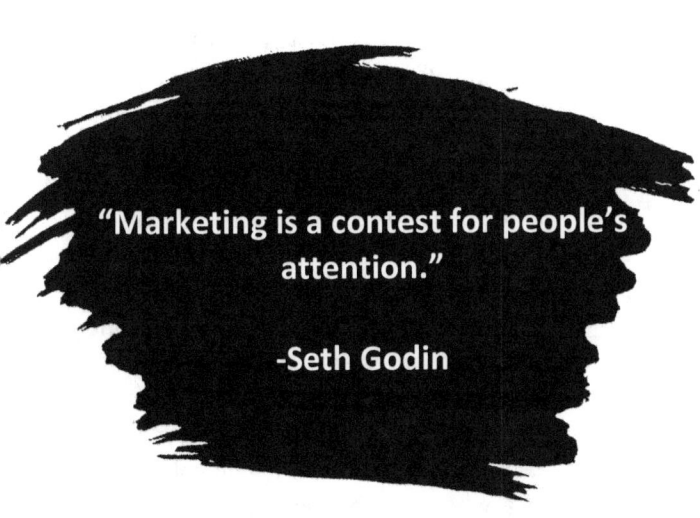

"Marketing is a contest for people's attention."

-Seth Godin

94 "Don't put too many irons in the fire"

95 "Keep your eye on the ball"

In the early days of your business, or perhaps for the whole life of it, it's probably just you or a very small group of people contributing towards the business. One person can only do so many things in a day. You have deadlines to meet, value to create, stats to track, emails to answer, and on top of everything else, you probably keep coming up with great new ideas for products or things that will make everything so much better or easier! Project envy and excitement can make it far too easy to take on extra projects and work, and while you may be able to accomplish them all, it will take a lot longer as a whole to complete every task and you will leave yourself more overwhelmed and stressed in the process.

Secondly, humans are notoriously good at overestimating their ability to multitask, even when multiple studies and the growing numbers of distracted driving accidents prove otherwise. You won't have as good of results focusing on multiple tasks as you would focusing on one.

You will get distracted, forget what you were doing, or forget details if you focus on too many things. Take things one at a time and you will complete them better and faster than otherwise.

"Concentrate all your thoughts upon the work in hand. The sun's rays do not burn until brought to a focus."

-Alexander Graham Bell

96 "A bad workman blames his tools"

As stated before, mistakes are going to happen. Maybe even more often than not at the beginning. Not only that, *not everything you touch is going to turn into gold*. Some things are going to turn out poorly. It's easy to say, "If I had had better tools, or if I had the latest and greatest thing, it would have worked better." And in some cases this may be true, however lack of quality in something usually results from lack of skill. A more skilled and knowledgeable person can do more with less!

There is a line of thought called the Dunning-Kreuger effect, which states that someone with lesser skill and knowledge will greatly overestimate their abilities than someone who knows better. Basically, people don't know what they don't know! Instead of trying to push blame onto something else (which gets you absolutely nowhere anyways) accept that you're not perfect at everything and that there is more to learn! By acknowledging your shortcomings, you can better anticipate and work around them, whether it's subcontracting certain tasks out, revising how something is done, or avoiding some things altogether. Being accountable to yourself actually creates forward progress!

"If you do what you've always done, you'll get what you've always gotten."

-Tony Robbins

97 "A bird in hand is worth two in the bush"

It can be easy to get starry eyed with the next big thing. Whether it's the shiny tools that will make your life so much easier, or the shiny new office space your competitor just got, envy of what you don't have can be crippling (and unnecessarily expensive). Just because you don't have the most optimal situation at your disposal doesn't mean you can't do great work with what you have. Sure, it might take a little more time and effort, but by focusing on what you have and what your strengths are in your current situation and then employing them can still get you where you want to go. You might even find that by working with what you have vs what you don't, you can complete tasks faster and end up with better solutions, without spending money needed to make things "perfect."

If you're stuck because you think you're lacking something that you can't afford, maybe it's time to take a step back, reevaluate, and plot a new course to your destination.

98 "Laugh and the world laughs with you, weep and you weep alone"

In marketing and social media, many businesses often have a voice or tone that they employ. With many small businesses, especially single person businesses, that voice is controlled by the entrepreneur themselves. It is important to remember that this voice is how many customers interact with a business.

With the many trials and tribulations, a one-man business goes through, you must be sure not to vent and take it out on customers, no matter how frustrating. Customers do care about the businesses they support and will understand some issues a business may be going through, and they will most likely want to hear about major hurdles as well, but nobody likes a Debbie downer, and customer pity won't get you far. People want positive vibes in their feeds and will quickly drop a company who is complaining too much. Issues may be extraordinarily frustrating, but ultimately, they are yours to bear, not the customers.

99

"You can lead a horse to water, but you can't make him drink it"

You might have spent hours and hours crafting the most meticulous advertising description, come up with the best imagery, the most amazing marketing idea to show off your stellar, brilliant product, and yet still people don't want to buy it. This happens to every business out there both big and small. Sometimes the market just isn't geared to accept certain things, no matter how amazing they are. Discouraging as it may be, sometimes you'll have to stow away something amazing, accept the losses incurred, and try a something else. And maybe someday the market will be ready, but keep trying!

"A good teacher will lead the horse to water, an excellent teacher will make the horse thirsty first."

-Mario Cortes

100 "There's no such thing as a free lunch"

If you want success as an entrepreneur, if you want to run your own business, if you want to get your dream job, you're going to have to go out there and get it. Nobody else is going to do it for you. Nobody is going to gift you your dreams. You're not entitled to it! You have to work harder, longer, smarter than everyone else. You must earn it!

So why are still reading this? Get going!

Credit where credit is due:

I would like to thank Austin Kleon and his books "Steal Like an Artist" and "Show your Work" for inspiring me to write this.

Also, thanks to EF Education (Education First) for their large lists of idioms.

And last, but not least, thank you everyone who has supported me on my own entrepreneurial journeys thus far!

-Jeremy

Since you're an entrepreneur, you wear many hats. If one of them deals with design, check out my other book: "Contrast – Intro to Designing Beyond Form & Function."

No matter what it is you design, architecture, products, interiors, websites, you name it, this book has value for you.

Available at www.Brace.Design or on the Google Play Book Store.

Shameless self-promotion:

...and on that topic, check out my business: BRACE Design where thoughtful design is merged with exceptional execution.

If you like stand-out watches, cool accessories, and comfy, ethical clothing options, check us out.

BRACE Yourself – quality is contagious.

www.Brace.Design

About the Author

I am an engineer, designer, and serial entrepreneur. I love to make things. Occasionally some of these things are books.

See what I'm up to on Instagram @jerskoog
Or my blog: www.somanyhobbies.com

Being an entrepreneur is hard, and it's a lot of work...

...Fortunately, many people have gone ahead of you and learned about it, and they've got lessons to share with you! Languages are amazing in that they not only provide direct—face value meaning. But also provide indirect lessons and values that we can learn from, embedded in the language itself! These are IDIOMS, and we use them all the time to easily transfer knowledge down...

...if you can decipher it.

That's why this book exists, to translate important entrepreneurial knowledge to you in the form of memorable idioms!